Undersea Exploration

Contents	Page

written by John Lockyer

From space, Earth looks like a watery blue ball. It is the only planet in the Solar System that has liquid oceans. The Arctic, Pacific, Atlantic, Indian and Southern Oceans cover more than two-thirds of Earth's surface. They are the planet's main environment, but people have explored only a small part of them. In fact, more humans have flown to the moon than have been down to the deepest place in the ocean!

Scientists have divided the oceans into five zones:

1. The **sunlit zone**, about 650 feet/200 metres below the surface, has changing temperatures with plenty of light and sea life.
2. Under that, down to 3,300 feet/1,000 m, is the **twilight zone**. Animals there have just enough light for hunting.
3. Beyond that depth is the **dark zone** where there is no light, so some animals make bioluminescent light to attract prey.
4. Further down is the **abyssal zone** – to 20,000 feet/6,000 m.
5. Deeper still is the **hadal zone** – to 33,000 feet/10,000m.

These are the deepest places on Earth.

Before early explorers could explore the ocean, they had to work
out how to breathe underwater and how to cope with water
pressure.

In 1690, a diving bell was built out of wood. It was watertight
at the top and had an opening at the bottom. The diver sat on a
seat above the opening. When the bell was lowered into the sea,
air pressure kept the water out of the inside. The diver was able
to explore the sea bed by wearing a helmet that was connected to
the diving bell by an air pipe.

Diving suits were developed in the 1830s. Made of waterproof canvas, rubber and metal, they allowed people to dive to around 196 feet/60 metres.

When scuba (self-contained underwater breathing apparatus) was invented, divers reached depths of about 475 feet/145 metres.

Modern newtsuits are made of metal and are pressure-proof. They give divers the ability to go down to 2,000 feet/600 metres for up to 8 hours. Newtsuits have flexible joints and thrusters so divers can move about freely.

Submarines were developed to take explorers deeper underwater. Submarines carry their own food, fuel and air. The first submarine was the *Turtle*. Built in 1776, it had room for one person. To go down, water was let into the bottom of the craft. To go up, the water was pumped out by hand. Hand-cranked propellers moved the *Turtle* forward or backward. The *Turtle* could stay underwater for thirty minutes. Today, modern nuclear submarines can stay submerged for months.

Submersible launch

Submersibles are smaller than submarines. They are launched
from a mother ship which supplies the craft with fuel, power and
air. In 1934, a round steel chamber called a bathysphere was
lowered 3,280 feet/1,000 metres underwater. The diver used a
telephone to report what he saw from the porthole.

In the 1950s, a much deeper diving submersible called *Trieste* reached 10,300 feet/3,139 metres. In 1960, the U.S. Navy improved the *Trieste* so it could drop into the deepest place on Earth – Challenger Deep. At Challenger Deep, the weight of the ocean above is massive. It is the same as a person trying to hold 50 jumbo jets!

Challenger Deep is in
the Mariana Trench in
the Pacific Ocean. It is
7 miles/11 kilometres
below the ocean's surface.
It took the *Trieste* five
hours to reach the
bottom of the trench.
The divers stayed there
for 20 minutes before
returning to the surface.
In 2012, the filmmaker
James Cameron made a
solo dive to Challenger
Deep aboard a small
submersible shaped like
a torpedo. It took him
two and a half hours to
reach the ocean floor.
He took photographs and
videos, then collected
sea bed samples before
returning to the surface.

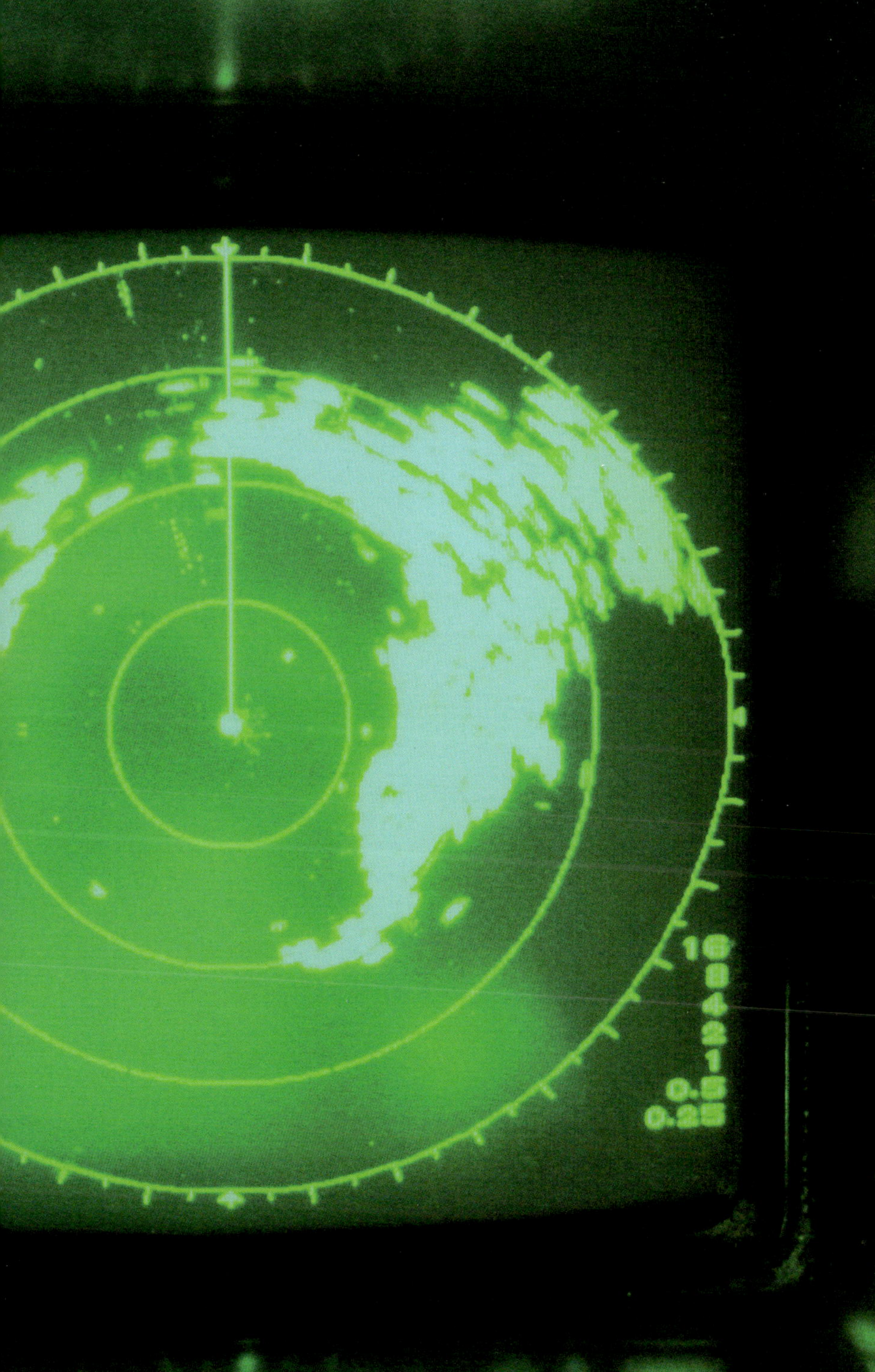
16
0
4
2
1
0.5
0.25

The U.S. Navy uses a submersible called *Alvin* for deep dives.
Alvin can carry two scientists and a pilot. Since 1964, it has
made more than 4,500 dives. Most dives last up to ten hours.
Alvin was used to locate a lost hydrogen bomb. Scientists aboard
Alvin discovered the first of many hydrothermal vents, which are
hot springs like underwater geysers.

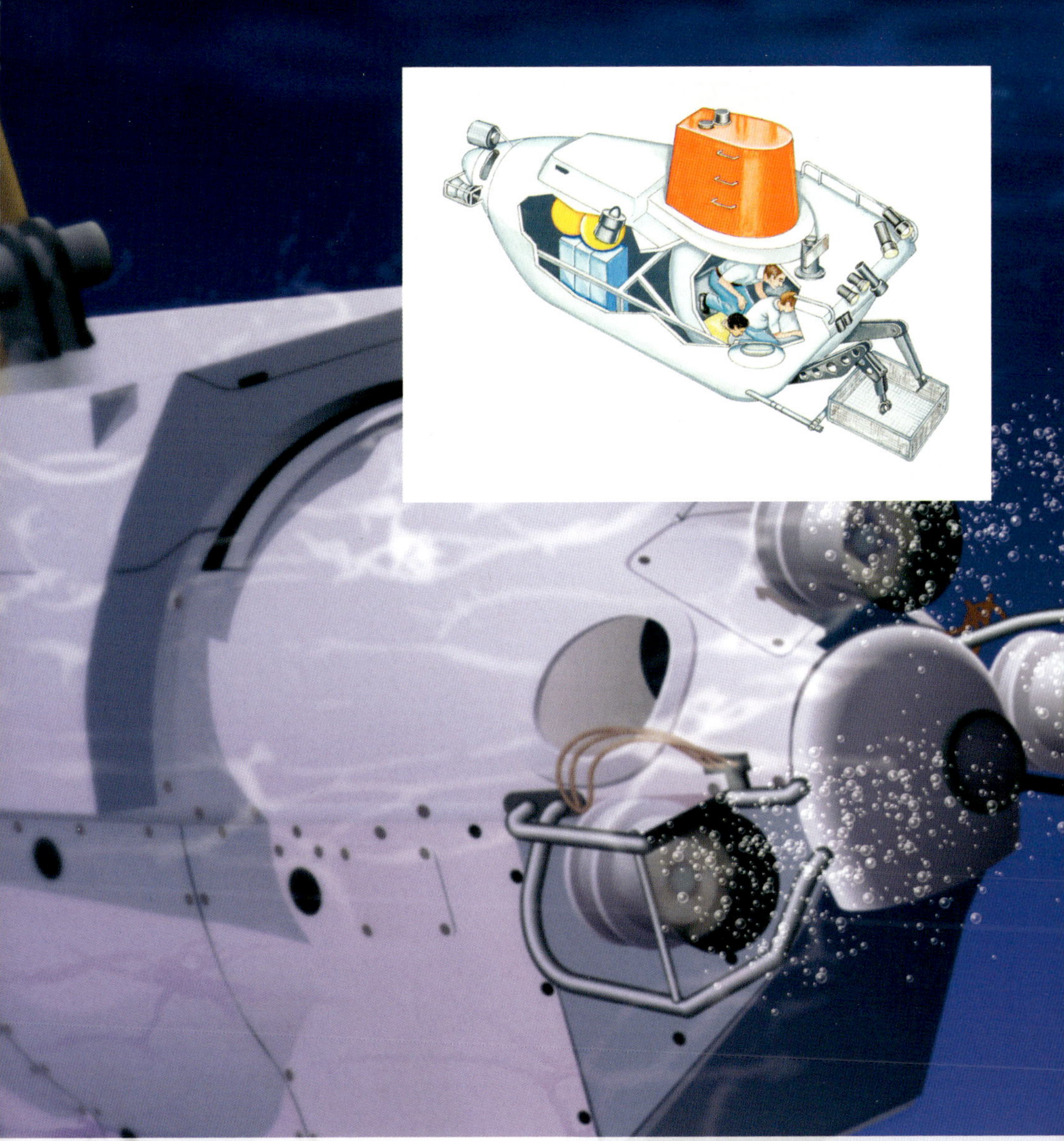

The submersible was also used to inspect the *Titanic* wreck.
Alvin is equipped with cameras, robotic arms and a basket that
can carry up to 1,500 pounds/680 kilograms. In the future, *Alvin*
will be upgraded to dive to 19,700 feet/6,000 metres.

The French submersible, *Nautile*, has similar equipment to the *Alvin*. It has space for three people and can stay underwater for eight hours. Whenever it does a deep dive, its extra-thick, curved portholes are squeezed flat by water pressure. *Nautile* has been used to discover sunken ships and plane wrecks.

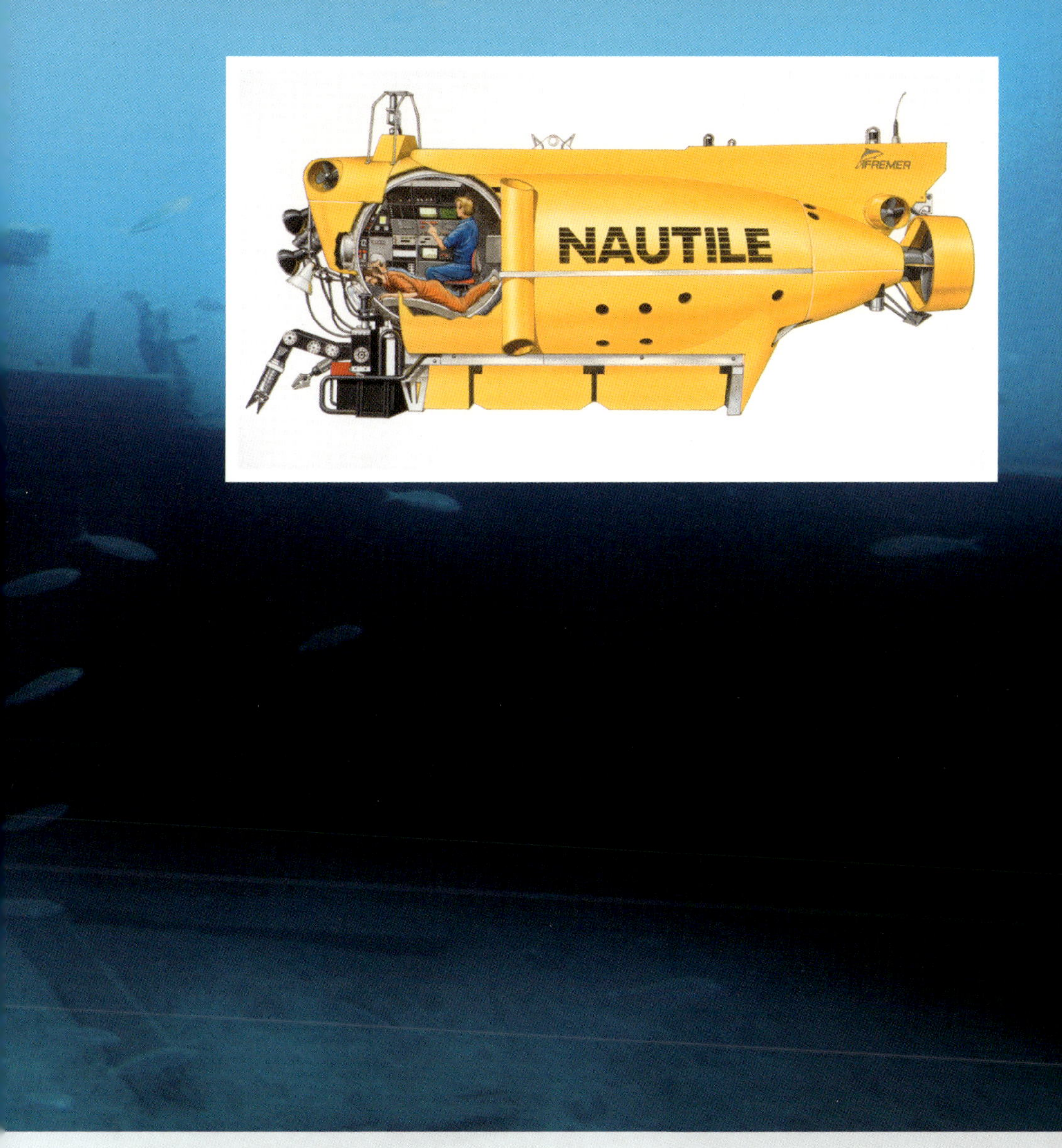

ROVs – or Remotely Operated Vehicles – are often used to explore the ocean when the conditions are dangerous. Operators on a mother ship control these unmanned vessels. They are ideal for investigating inside wrecks and caves or beneath the polar ice.

The ROV *Jason*, is
used for exploring
hydrothermal vents
on the ocean floor.
Operator instructions
and power are delivered
to the ROV through a 6
mile/10 kilometre cable.
Jason is fitted with
imagers, cameras and
manipulator arms. Most
dives last around 21
hours, but *Jason* can stay
underwater for four days.
AUVs – or Autonomous
Underwater Vehicles – are
used to explore remote
oceans like the Arctic
and Antarctic. AUVs are
unmanned and operate
without cables. *Autosub*
is a torpedo-shaped AUV.
It is fitted with biological
and chemical sensors.
The sensors tell scientists
what is happening in the
ocean.

Over the years, explorers – with the help of machines and technology – have made many discoveries below the ocean's surface: huge mountain ranges, volcanoes, flat plains and deep trenches. They have recovered man-made objects from shipwrecks and sunken cities; new creatures and plants have been photographed. They have collected sea bed samples that have shown what ancient Earth was like. But there is still more to explore and more to discover in this vast wilderness. Who knows what mysteries the ocean still holds?

EXPERIMENTAL RESEARCH